HELPING THE COURT DECIDE

Report of an Inspection of
Social Enquiry Reports
for the Criminal Courts

Social Work Services Inspectorate for Scotland

1996

Purpose and responsibilities

Our purpose is to work with others to continually improve social work services so that:

- they genuinely meet people's needs; and

- the public has confidence in them.

The Social Work Services Inspectorate
James Craig Walk
Edinburgh
EH1 3BA

FOREWORD

Preparing social enquiry reports demands a high standard of professional practice. It requires skilled interviewing, the ability to collect and assess information from different sources, and the art of writing a report which is dependable, constructive, impartial and brief.

In this inspection we found some good practice but also considerable room for improvement. We concluded that:

- writers should face offenders more with the impact of their crime on the victim,

- more attention should be given to assessing risk factors,

- writers should be more cogent in presenting their arguments, and

- ways should be found to provide the service more efficiently.

Our recommendations are intended to help bring about improvements in these areas. Some can be addressed straightaway by local authorities, others require revisiting national standards and some the assistance of the Judiciary and criminal justice agencies.

In the end each sentence is an individual act and the quality of justice rests finally on the personal and professional skill of the judge or magistrate. The same applies to social workers who carry a personal responsibility for the standard of each report and for the assistance it gives the court in reaching a decision. Every social worker writing reports should consider the issues in this report and how to ensure they personally provide a consistently high quality of service. All social workers in the criminal justice field will have access to the report and each will be provided with a summary.

ANGUS SKINNER
Chief Inspector of Social Work Services for Scotland

CONTENTS

Chapter 1

Introduction

1.1   This inspection was about the quality of the social enquiry reports which Scottish local authority social work departments provide to the criminal courts. The provision of social enquiry reports is covered by legislation[1] and by national objectives and standards[2].

1.2   We inspected the quality of social enquiry reports for two reasons. First, they account for a significant proportion of the resources allocated to criminal justice social work services as a whole. It was therefore important to consider whether the service was as effective and efficient as possible. Second, they act as an important link between judicial decision making and those community based disposals which local authorities supervise on behalf of the courts. We wanted to examine how this link worked in practice and to assess the extent to which the information and advice contained in social enquiry reports helped to achieve the objective set out in the national standards that the courts do not use custody for want of a suitable community based disposal.

1.3   A social enquiry report is a report about an offender which is made available to the court before sentence. Between April 1991 when national standards were introduced and the end of March 1995, a total of just over 108,000 reports were prepared at an estimated cost of £23,500,000.[3] This was around 25% of the total spent on criminal justice social work services over the same 4 years. The average cost per report for the financial year 1996-97 is estimated by SWSG[4] at £204.

1.4   The social workers who prepare these reports are based in local social work teams in the 12 regional and islands authorities (and will transfer to the 32 new authorities in April 1996). They are professionally qualified in social work and most specialise to some degree in providing social work services in the criminal justice system.

1.5   In undertaking the inspection we were assisted by four experienced criminal justice social work practitioners drawn from Scottish local authority social work departments and by two lay inspectors who played a full part in the inspection. We also had the benefit of advice from an inspection advisory group on which a wide range of interests was represented. Members of the inspection team and the advisory group are listed at Appendix 1. A researcher also undertook a specific piece of work on behalf of the inspection team.

---

1. Discussed in Chapter 2
2. National Objectives and Standards for Social Work Services in the Criminal Justice System. The Scottish Office: Social Work Services Group: February 1991.
3. These costs included the costs of employing court-based social workers in some authorities.
4. The Social Work Services Group of The Scottish Office Home Department.

Method

1.6   We collected a sample of 410 full reports and 33 pre-trial reports prepared for courts throughout Scotland during selected weeks in September 1994. The weeks varied between regions and each region was given only short notice of the dates for collection to ensure as far as possible that the content of the reports was not influenced by their inclusion in the inspection. We analysed the 443 reports using a checklist based on the national standards for the preparation of reports. This provided detailed information about what the reports contained and enabled us to assess their quality. We examined the differences between reports prepared on different types of offender and categories of offence[5] and those reports which we evaluated as either "very good" or "poor".

1.7   Twenty-nine sentencers agreed to complete a questionnaire which enabled us to find out their views about the service they received. They comprised 20 permanent Sheriffs drawn from 4 Sheriff courts, 5 High Court Judges, 2 floating Sheriffs and 2 temporary Sheriffs. We conducted follow-up interviews with 7 permanent Sheriffs, one High Court Judge, one floating Sheriff and one temporary Sheriff.

1.8   To find out the views of social workers and managers responsible for providing the service, we carried out separate interviews with practitioners and their managers at those Sheriff Courts where permanent Sheriffs had been approached to participate in the inspection. We conducted these interviews in groups wherever possible. The size of the practitioner groups ranged from 5 to 10 and the manager groups from 2 to 6. Short interviews were also held with the senior managers responsible for the service.

1.9   We commissioned interviews with a self-selected sample of 30 offenders on whom reports had been prepared during the months of August and September 1994. An inspector or lay inspector attended most of these interviews.

1.10   We examined national statistics[6] about reports prepared between 1 January and 31 March 1994. These provide a range of information including information about the characteristics and previous offending histories of the subjects of reports. A profile of these offenders drawn from these statistics and our sample is included at Appendix 2.

This report

1.11   This report is set out in the following way. Chapter 2 deals with the legislative and policy context in which the service operates. Chapters 3-9 evaluate the service against seven important dimensions of quality. Chapter 10 identifies a number of key messages for the future. Chapter 11 adds the comments of our lay inspectors and lists our recommendations.

---

5. The types of offender and categories of offence were sex offenders; female offenders; offenders identified in reports as having either a current or previous mental health problem; cases of domestic violence: offenders between 16 and 20.
6. The National Core Data System established by the Scottish Office to collect information from every local authority about key aspects of criminal justice social work practice.

Chapter 2

The Requirements of the Law and National Standards

What the law says

2.1 The purposes of reports, who is responsible for preparing them and the circumstances in which reports can or must be obtained are set out in the Criminal Procedure (Scotland) Act 1995. The Act does not use the term 'social enquiry report' but this is how reports have come to be described.

2.2 Courts have a power to adjourn a case before sentence "for the purpose of enabling enquiries to be made or of determining the most suitable method for dealing with his case". This power is fleshed out by references to the provision of information about the offender's character and circumstances; the nature and circumstances of the offence; the suitability of the offender for named disposals and the availability of resources to supervise the offender in the community. Local authorities are identified as the main providers of reports. The clerk of the court must give a copy of any report prepared about an offender to the offender or his solicitor.

2.3 Reports must be available within 21 days where the offender is remanded in custody, or within 28 days where the offender is remanded on bail or ordained to appear[7]. Courts must obtain a report before making a probation, community service or supervised release order. A report is required before imposing sentences of detention or custody on offenders under 21, or on offenders aged 21 and over who have not previously been in custody. Reports must be obtained on offenders under the age of 16 who appear in court and on offenders up to the age of 18 who are subject to a children's hearing supervision requirement. From 1 April 1996, these categories extend to offenders appearing at court for disposal who are under current supervision by court order or following release from custody. These include offenders on probation and community service, offenders subject to a supervised release order and offenders released from detention on licence.

2.4 In the case of offenders under 21 and offenders aged 21 and over with no previous custodial sentences, the court must be satisfied, before imposing custody that no other method of dealing with the offender is appropriate. The report must cover the offender's circumstances, and the court must also take into account any information concerning the offender's character and physical and mental condition. In the case of a supervised release order, the court must decide whether to make an order at the point at which a custodial sentence is imposed if it considers such an order necessary to protect the public from serious

---

7. National standards require social work departments to provide reports on offenders remanded in custody within 14 days and offenders released on bail or ordained to appear within 21 days.

3

harm from the offender on release. The report must provide information about the offender and his or her circumstances and the court can, if necessary, hear the officer who prepared it.

What the law does not say

2.5   While it is clear that the purpose of social enquiry reports is to assist the court to decide what disposal to make, the law does not say how this should be done. For example, the law does not say whether or not it is appropriate for the authors of reports to comment on the suitability of offenders for probation (although it is explicit on this point for community service) or that the information provided can include advice to sentencers on factors they might wish to take into account. Nothing is said about whether or not it is appropriate to extend advice of this kind to include recommendations or proposals for a particular disposal. The law is clear that the information contained in reports should assist the court to decide whether there are ways of dealing with the offender in the community which enable the court to avoid the use of detention or custody - certainly in the case of all offenders up to 21 and all other offenders facing a first custodial sentence. Except for community service, the law does not require reports to comment on the feasibility or appropriateness of named community based disposals although this has been inferred from the law.

What the national standards say

The context

2.6   The Government introduced new arrangements for funding criminal justice social work services in April 1991. Under these arrangements, the full approved costs incurred by local authorities are met by Government, provided local authorities organise, manage and deliver these services according to national standards laid down by the Secretary of State[8]. The Standards set out objectives, priorities and standards for providing social enquiry reports within the context of Government policy for other criminal justice social work services, notably community service and probation. The standards contain extensive guidance on how to prepare and write reports including those aspects of practice on which the law is silent.

2.7   A main aim of Government policy for criminal justice social work services as set out in the national standards is to seek to ensure that courts do not have to impose a custodial sentence for want of an appropriate community based disposal. A key objective of criminal justice social work services is therefore to provide community based disposals which have the confidence of the courts and the wider public. Sentencers must know that these disposals are available in sufficient quality and quantity and be clear about what service will be provided when they make an order. National standards and 100% funding were introduced by Government to achieve this.

---

8. Footnote 1 refers.

Key service objectives

2.8   The national standards state that social enquiry reports should assist sentencing and act as the main link between the court and the services which local authorities and other agencies make available to deal with offenders in the community. They introduce an emphasis on offending behaviour in the preparation of reports which is not explicit in the law. According to the standards, reports should inform and advise the court on those aspects of an offender's circumstances and personality which have a bearing on their offending behaviour by:

- setting the subject's offending behaviour into a personal and social context;
- examining the subject's view of that behaviour;
- considering the likelihood of and scope for minimising future offending; and
- assessing the possible effects of the range of disposals available to the court on the subject and on any dependants[9].

2.9   The standards also state that part of the purpose of a report is to assess the offender's willingness to accept responsibility for his or her criminal behaviour and its consequences, and his or her capacity to take steps to deal with it. Reports should therefore comment on the offender's view of the impact of the offence on the victim and may offer a view as to whether the offender could make direct reparation to the victim[10].

2.10   The standards require authors of reports to concentrate on making feasible community based options available to the court, particularly those involving social work resources. If the author has a preferred option he or she is encouraged to say so[11]. The clear aim is to assist the court to consider whether these options are appropriate, even in more serious cases where custody is likely. Where the court requests a report on an offender who almost inevitably faces custody because of the seriousness of the present offence or because of previous serious or persistent offending, the standards indicate that the author should nevertheless advise on whether a community based option is feasible at least for offenders under 21 and for those offenders over 20 facing their first term of imprisonment[12].

2.11   A report which recommends or proposes a probation order should include an action plan which makes clear what the offender will be required to do and what services can be made available to work with him or her to reduce the risk of re-offending.

Other objectives

2.12   The national standards identify a number of other objectives related to improving the quality of the report; increasing the chances of a successful outcome if the court decides on a community based disposal; and working with the offender before sentence to begin to tackle his or her offending or associated difficulties. Local authorities must pursue these

---

9. National Standards, Part 2, Social Enquiry and Related Reports and Associated Court Services, paragraph 6.
10. National Standards, Part 2, paragraphs 10. 12 and 14.
11. National Standards, Part 2, paragraph 93.
12. Criminal Justice (Scotland) Act 1980, Sections 42 and 45; National Standards, Part 2, paragraph 87.

objectives wherever the circumstances of the case indicate[13]. They are to:

- engage with the offender and seek to motivate and encourage active participation in facing up to his or her behaviour and in considering its consequences;

- carry out an assessment which may provide a basis for future social work action;

- begin to negotiate a specific course of action to address problems and issues associated with offending behaviour;

- explain to the offender what will be involved in any action plan which may be put to the court and seek his or her informed consent;

- explain to the offender the range of uses to which a social enquiry report may be put and the boundaries of confidentiality; and

- explain to the offender that the final decision rests with the court.

These objectives mean that in some cases, social workers offer a service to the offender during the period between conviction and sentence in addition to the work required to prepare the report.

Service priorities

2.13 The standards encourage local authorities to concentrate on those offenders who are at risk of custody, are likely to re-offend, or, in the case of young people, might better be dealt with by the children's hearings. The Secretary of State issues an annual statement of national priorities which local authorities must take into account in preparing the following year's service plan. Between 1992 and 1995, the Secretary of State gave high priority to:

- providing social enquiry and related reports as required by the courts and in compliance with national standards;

- concentrating the use of community service to the fullest extent possible on those offenders at immediate risk of custody; and

- targeting probation supervision to the fullest extent possible on those offenders at immediate risk of custody, who constitute a serious risk of re-offending, and who are aged between 16 and 20 years.

According to these priorities, the authors of reports are expected to concentrate on assessing the feasibility of community based disposals involving social work resources, for those offenders at risk of immediate custody and further offending, especially young adults. The national standards encourage local authorities to discuss the scope for reducing the demand for social enquiry reports with sentencers, where reports are not required by law and the offender appears on a minor charge or is a first or early offender. In this way maximum benefit should be achieved at least cost, by targeting resources on offenders most at risk of custody. The standards state that any service offered to the court involving the use of social work services should be based on the principle of the minimum necessary intervention[14].

---

13. National Standards, Part 2, paragraphs 16.1-16.6.
14. National Standards, Part 2, paragraph 9.

They remind local authorities that the services which they can provide are not limited to those criminal justice social work services currently funded by central Government[15].

Who is the customer and who should provide the service?

2.14 The national standards state that it is not any purpose of a report to represent the offender or to mitigate on his or her behalf[16]. The clear intention is that social enquiry reports are a service for the courts and not for offenders. Social enquiry reports are only one source of information and advice available to the court in deciding the most suitable method of dealing with a particular case[17]. Judgements about guilt or innocence, public disapproval and deterrence are matters for the court, not for those preparing social enquiry reports[18].

Good practice

2.15 National standards state that good practice involves advising the court about the feasibility of community based sentencing options like community service and probation. This advice should include an assessment of the risk of re-offending and what might be done in the community to reduce or prevent future offending. The standards see the preparation of a social enquiry report as an opportunity:

- for offenders - to consider the reasons for their offending behaviour and do something about them;

- for social workers - to consider with the offender whether there are ways they can make reparation and whether they are motivated to address their offending and any problems associated with it; and

- for the court - to consider whether a community based sentence can be imposed which enables the offender to make reparation and which can assist in preventing or reducing future offending.

2.16 National standards require that this work is only undertaken by qualified social workers because of the complex nature of the task and the responsibilities involved[19].

CONCLUSIONS

2.17 Taken together, the law and national standards enable social enquiry reports to contribute to sentencing decisions and, by addressing the risk of re-offending, to inform the court's consideration of issues of public safety. This contribution will be maximised if sentencers are satisfied with the quality of the service and well informed and confident about the quality of the programmes of supervision. Hence the importance which national standards attach to local arrangements for exchanging information and for dialogue between local authorities and sentencers[20]. However, the situation is not straightforward.

---

15. National Standards, Part 2, paragraphs 72-76.
16. National Standards, Part 2, paragraphs 3 and 4.
17. National Standards, Part 2, paragraph 5.
18. National Standards, Part 2, paragraphs 87 and 93.
19. National Standards, Part 2, paragraph 6.
20. National Standards, Part 1, paragraphs 107-110.

Local authorities must comply with Government policy and national standards whilst sentencers are bound solely by the law. In the case of social enquiry reports, the law offers sentencers the scope to determine their own information needs by giving local authorities a responsibility to make available to the court "such social background reports and other reports ..... which the court may require for disposal of a case"[21].

2.18 There is therefore room for differences of view between sentencers and social workers on such crucial issues as whether social enquiry reports ought to address the risk of re-offending, the appropriateness of offering advice and the form this should take. These stem from the generality of the law, the constitutional separation of the judiciary from Government and the specificity of government policy, priorities and standards. They are translated at local level into differing expectations about what should be included in reports and differing views about the quality of the service, not only between sentencers and local authorities, but also between individual sentencers. These issues are taken up in following chapters of this report.

---

21. Social Work (Scotland) Act 1968, Section 27(1).

Chapter 3

How Clear are the Purposes of Social Enquiry Reports in Practice?

The law

3.1   The main purpose of a social enquiry report in law is to provide information about the offender and his or her circumstances to assist the court in determining the most suitable method of dealing with the case. Where the offender is aged between 16 and 20, or is over 21 and facing the possibility of a first custodial sentence, social enquiry reports are intended to assist the court in reaching a view as to whether a disposal other than custody may be appropriate. Social enquiry reports have no other purpose in law than to serve the needs of sentencers. They are only one of a number of information sources available to the court and do not address all the factors which the court takes into account when sentencing.

Sentencers

3.2   The **sentencers** interviewed saw the purpose of social enquiry reports as being to inform sentencing decisions by providing information about the offender and his or her circumstances. With only a few exceptions, they made it clear that information in this context included not just factual information but also:

- **analysis,** for example, analysing a possible association between offending and substance misuse;

- **comment,** for example, commenting on the implications of an identified health problem for disposal; and

- **advice on disposal,** for example, advising on the feasibility of different disposals, especially those involving social work services.

They needed up-to-date information and saw the social enquiry report as a valuable source of this. They generally considered that advice about the feasibility of community based disposals could help them identify ways of sentencing which were worthwhile provided that such advice was balanced, objective, realistic and recognised the court's wider responsibilities for sentencing. Most indicated that they saw part of the purpose of a report as addressing offending behaviour, but had different views about what this should cover. These included possible reasons for offending, the risk of harm to others, the risk of re-offending, the offender's motivation and capacity to change.

3.3   About half those interviewed considered that social workers held the same views as themselves about the purpose of social enquiry reports, and that this was increasingly so. However, about one third thought that social workers saw the purpose of social enquiry reports as representing the offender in some way, for example, as a means of deflecting sentencers from imposing heavier penalties, particularly custody. One sentencer felt this approach could lead to unrealistic recommendations and undermine the credibility of social enquiry reports. Another thought that social workers saw social enquiry reports as a means of persuading courts to use social work disposals, another that social workers were not always clear about the purposes of reports.

Social workers

3.4   The **social workers** interviewed held much the same views as sentencers, although they placed more emphasis on the social enquiry report as a means of examining offending behaviour and a source of advice on the feasibility of community based disposals, especially those involving social work services. They believed that the views of sentencers coincided with their own, although some social workers thought that, for some sentencers, the purpose of a social enquiry report depended on the circumstances of the particular case. The examples they gave included meeting the requirements of statute, avoiding an appeal, or because they were undecided about what to do and wanted more information.

3.5   Both social workers and their managers considered that they had responsibilities to the subjects of social enquiry reports as well as to the courts. While they described the court variously as "the customer", "the primary customer" or "the primary stakeholder", they often described the subject of the report as "the client" or "the secondary customer". Most saw offenders as the recipients of a service when reports were prepared on them. The main purpose of this service was to do justice to offenders in the sense of being accurate in what they said about them and their circumstances, being fair to their situation, and helping them understand the sentencing process. It was also part of their purpose to help offenders help themselves and begin to tackle offence related problems. They judged such activity appropriate in its own right. It also helped offenders to improve their prospects when they appeared for sentence and, where a report proposed probation, prepared the ground in the event of a probation order being made.

3.6   Both **sentencers and social workers** agreed that offenders saw social enquiry reports as a means of getting themselves off as lightly as possible. Neither had any illusions about the propensity of offenders to reduce or deny responsibility for their own behaviour and to use social workers to obtain whatever advantage they could. Some social workers felt that, while some offenders saw the social enquiry report as a means of having their voice heard in court and obtaining a fair deal, most simply did not think about its purpose or, if they did, had confused notions and simply acquiesced.

Offenders

3.7   Most of the **offenders** interviewed thought that the main purpose of reports was to supply background information about them: what kind of people they were. Almost a third said they did not know what the purpose of a social enquiry report was and very few thought it was concerned with addressing their offending. The authors of reports appeared to be the persons most likely to provide information about their purpose although from the accounts of offenders they did not appear to give much emphasis to offending. Most offenders either did not receive, or did not absorb, information about the purpose of the report from the Sheriff or the court social worker. Only one third remembered having been seen by a court social worker at the time a report was requested. Less than half recollected having received a leaflet from the social work department outlining the purpose of the report in advance. Defence agents were more often cited as providing information about the purpose of a report than either Sheriffs or court based social workers.

CONCLUSIONS

3.8   There was a measure of agreement between sentencers and social workers about the general purposes of reports but some differences about how these should be translated into practice both between sentencers and between sentencers and social workers. Social workers placed more emphasis on assessing offending behaviour and the feasibility of community based sentencing options. We think that this reflects the differences between the generality of the law and the specificity of government policy, priorities and standards which we identified in the previous chapter.

3.9   We agree with the position taken in the national standards that assessing offending behaviour is part of the purpose of a social enquiry report. Only by doing so can the authors offer sound advice about what might be achieved by any disposal to reduce offending and harm to others. Not surprisingly, High Court Judges questioned the value of pre-trial reports for this reason[22]. The point at issue is how this should apply in practice.

3.10   In commenting on the feasibility of community based sentencing options, report writers are again following the guidance set out in the national standards. Sentencers are not in any way bound by these standards and for them, the social enquiry report is only one of a number of information sources and addresses only some of those factors which they must take into account at sentence. Sentencers and social workers have distinct roles and responsibilities in the sentencing process. The role of the social worker is to assist the court in reaching a decision about the most appropriate sentence. It is difficult to see how this role can be fulfilled to a consistently high standard unless there is more general agreement about how it should be carried out.

3.11   In providing advice on the feasibility of community based sentencing options, social workers must avoid describing their relationship to the subjects of reports in ways which may give the impression that reports are prepared on behalf of the offender. The social worker's responsibility is to provide impartial information and objective advice and the sentencer should never gain the impression that this requirement is secondary to other concerns. Social workers must distinguish clearly between the tasks of advising the court and helping the offender. Holding this distinction may not be easy but is vital to maintaining the court's confidence in the impartiality of reports.

3.12   Many offenders approach their initial contact with the social worker knowing little about what to expect. Because of this they may resent anything they perceive as an intrusion and be less honest about themselves than they otherwise might be. This hampers the social worker's efforts to obtain accurate information and reach informed conclusions.

---

22. See below, paragraph 9.7.

3.13 It is unwise for social workers to assume that offenders know why social enquiry reports are being prepared or understand what is involved, even if they have been the subject of a report before or have had the purpose of the report explained to them by the Sheriff or a court based social worker. It is also unwise to expect that defence agents will explain accurately what is involved. Social workers should always explain to the offender what a report is, why the court needs it and how the job of the social worker is different from the job of the defence agent and the court. Managers should check regularly the extent to which the subjects of reports understand their purpose as part of local arrangements for monitoring service quality.

Defining the purpose of social enquiry reports

3.14 We think that the main purpose of the social enquiry report is to provide information and advice which assist the court to sentence the offender in the most appropriate way, taking account of all the circumstances. A good report will provide a brief description of the offender and his or her circumstances and will make a particular contribution to assessing:

- the offender's attitude towards his or her offending and motivation and capacity to change;
- the risk of future offending and harm to others;
- the feasibility of a community based disposal and in particular disposals involving supervision by local authority staff, even in more serious cases where custody is likely; and
- the need for supervision on the offender's release from custody where this could contribute to reducing the risk to public safety.

RECOMMENDATIONS

3.15 When national standards are next reviewed, members of the judiciary should be consulted about how the general purposes of social enquiry reports should be translated into practice.

3.16 Local authorities should make sure that social workers:

- send every offender on whom a report is requested a leaflet about the purpose of a social enquiry report and what is involved;
- explain to offenders what reports are for and that they include an assessment of offending behaviour and what can be done to reduce the risk of further offending and harm to others; and
- check that offenders understand.

3.17 Local authorities should give members of the legal profession likely to act as defence agents the same information about reports that they give to offenders.

Chapter 4

How relevant to sentencing is the information and advice contained in Social Enquiry Reports?

4.1   We asked sentencers (by questionnaire and interview) about the extent to which they found the information and advice contained in reports relevant to sentencing. The questions and answers fell into two main categories - the relevance of information and advice about the subject and his or her circumstances: and the relevance of information and advice about the subject's current offence and history of previous offending.

Information and advice about the offender and his or her circumstances

4.2   **Sentencers** said that the social enquiry report was their main vehicle for obtaining information about the offender and his or her circumstances. The report should give them a sense of the person they were dealing with. The wide range of information which national standards indicate should be considered for inclusion in reports was potentially helpful and the items of information singled out by the standards to be covered in every report were important, particularly information about physical and mental health, income, expenditure and disposable income. The helpfulness of the information beyond what was necessary to paint a brief picture of the subject depended on whether they could see its relevance to the sentencing decision. There was a tendency for reports to include some items of information routinely without pointing up their relevance. This was particularly true of information about schooling and early family history.

4.3   Figure 1 below shows the percentage of the 410 full reports which included information about the listed items. The bar chart shows that reports did not always include items of information required by national standards. This was particularly true of references to mental health and disposable income:

Figure 1: Items of information in Social Enquiry Reports—the percentage of reports which contained information about (N=410)

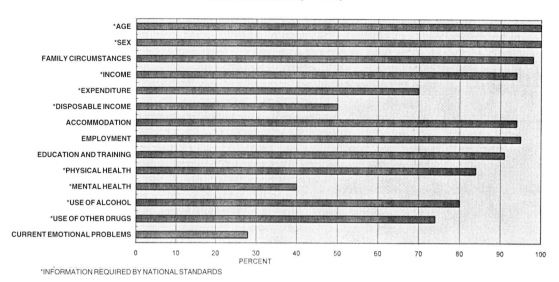

*INFORMATION REQUIRED BY NATIONAL STANDARDS

4.4   We examined the extent to which the authors drew inferences from the following items:

Table 1: The extent to which inferences were drawn when the following items of information were referred to in reports (expressed as a percentage)

Item of Information	% of reports which referred to item (N=410)	% of those reports which drew an inference	% of those reports which drew no inference	Unclear
Income and Expenditure	70 (287)	61	38	1
Use of Alcohol	80 (328)	52	46	2
Employment	95 (389)	41	47	2
Accommodation	94 (385)	35	63	2
Physical Health	83 (344)	30	68	2
Education and Training	92 (377)	16	82	2
Mental Health	30 (123)	43	45	2

When report writers included these items of information they did not necessarily draw any inferences from them, showing that a considerable amount of the information supplied was purely descriptive. We did not examine whether inferences or conclusions were drawn from clusters of items of information. However, the finding supports a later finding that a major weakness of a significant number of reports was the absence of much analytic content (see paragraph 8.7).

14

4.5   We also examined reports to see whether they made any inferences or drew any conclusions about "significant relationships". Our analysis showed that practitioners were more likely to make inferences and draw conclusions about this aspect of information than any other (72% of all full reports).

4.6   Only a small number of reports suggested that the court should obtain further information or advice about the offender and his or her circumstances before sentence. These suggestions were more likely in cases of domestic violence or where a current or previous mental health problem was identified.

4.7   **Practitioners** said they used the national standards to guide their decisions about what to investigate. They were aware that the standards required them to cover certain topics and said that these were always investigated although practice varied as to whether they always referred to them in reports. They appreciated both the need for information to be relevant and the responsibility to draw conclusions where these could be justified. They thought, however, that there was a place in reports for "free-standing" information. Some said that they included information about early family history because this was how they had been taught to carry out an assessment during their training. Some made the distinction between the information they needed to make an assessment and the information they needed to include in a report.

4.8   Almost one third of the **offenders** interviewed challenged the relevance of some of the questions which they were asked about themselves and their circumstances, particularly questions about their family background or current relationships. They also questioned the relevance of information about health and previous convictions. They expressed concern about social workers being "nosy" and prying too much into their personal lives.

CONCLUSIONS

4.9   Practitioners should always distinguish between the information they collect to make an assessment and the information they decide to include in a report. Sentencers want sufficient information about the subject and his or her circumstances to provide a context and they particularly value information about the subject's health and income. Beyond this, items of information are helpful to the extent that the report demonstrates their relevance. This does not mean that practitioners should not investigate other areas but it does mean that they should think carefully about why they are including certain items of information. The fact that inferences and conclusions were often hard to find suggests that practitioners were not doing this sufficiently.

4.10   The national standards require the inclusion of information and advice about the offender's income, expenditure, disposable income, physical and mental health and use of alcohol and other drugs. These items were not always referred to in reports although practitioners said they were covered at interview. The national standards are right to emphasise the importance of these items. The offender's income and necessary expenditure is critical to whether he or she is in a position to pay a financial penalty (the most common court disposal); information about physical and mental health is relevant to a range of possible disposals including community service and custody; information about the offender's use of alcohol and other drugs is relevant because of the well-established association between alcohol and other drug misuse and both health and offending.

4.11 **Reports should always refer to these items in a relevant way.** Telling the court that the offender says that he or she has no health problems or does not misuse alcohol is of limited value. Wherever possible, practitioners should offer an assessment of the offender's account, drawing on their interview(s) with the offender and any other available information. For this, practitioners will need to probe the statements which offenders make and not necessarily take them at face value. The interviews with offenders showed that they tended to minimise their use of alcohol and other drugs. With regard to health, social workers will need actively to screen for health factors which may have implications for sentence. When necessary they should not hold back from checking information with a doctor or from suggesting that the court obtains a medical or psychiatric report.

RECOMMENDATIONS

4.12 **Practitioners should explain to the subjects of reports why they are asking them questions about themselves and their circumstances.**

4.13 **Local authorities should ensure that the staff who prepare reports are appropriately trained to:**

- **interview offenders about their finances, their health, their use of alcohol and other drugs; and**

- **use this information in a relevant way in reports.**

INFORMATION AND ADVICE ABOUT OFFENDING BEHAVIOUR

4.14 The court normally requests a report after conviction. Offenders' attitudes towards their offending, possible explanations for it and the risks associated with possible future offending are therefore highly relevant to the court's consideration of what to do. For example, it is important for the court to know whether the offender accepts any responsibility for his or her actions and whether he or she shows concern for any victim.

4.15 National standards make it clear that reports should provide information relevant to understanding the subject's offending. We checked the information and advice about the current offence, any previous offending and the risk of re-offending which reports contained. Table 2 shows the extent to which the sample of 410 full reports provided information relevant to understanding the subject's offending.

Table 2: The extent to which reports provided information relevant to understanding offending: (N = 410)

Information about the current offence:	Whether included (as a percentage)		
	Yes	*No*	*Unclear*
What he or she did	80%	19%	1%
Its seriousness	50%	49%	1%
Its consequences for him or herself	24%	75%	1%
Its consequences for others	52%	46%	2%
Its impact on the victim	24%	74%	2%
Previous offending:			
	Yes	*No*	*Unclear*
Extent of previous offending	74%	25%	1%
Significance of previous offending	50%	46%	4%
Did the report comment on:			
	Yes	*No*	*Unclear*
Subject's view of re-offending	41%	56%	3%
Risk of re-offending	47%	51%	2%
Risk of re-offending involving possible harm to others	19%	75%	6%
The subject's response to any previous disposal	47%	49%	4%
Did the author of the report draw any conclusions about:			
	Yes	*No*	*Unclear*
Subject's views about what he/she did	52%	47%	1%
Subject's views about the seriousness of what he/she did	36%	63%	1%
Subject's motivation to stop re-offending	53%	45%	2%
Subject's capacity to stop re-offending	47%	52%	1%
The risk of re-offending	46%	53%	1%

4.16 This table shows that most, but not all reports included an account of the subject's views about what he or she did but were much less likely to deal with the subject's views about the seriousness of the offending and its consequences, including the consequences for any victim. Reports were much more likely to refer to the extent of any previous offending than to comment on its significance. The risk of re-offending was covered in less than one half of the sample of reports and the risk of re-offending involving possible harm to others was covered in slightly fewer than one in five reports. The extent to which practitioners drew conclusions about significant aspects of offending behaviour including the subject's motivation and capacity to stop offending ranged from just over one half to just over one third of all reports.

4.17 There were some marked differences in the way offending behaviour was dealt with depending on the nature of the offence. For example, reports prepared on offenders who had committed sexual offences and offences involving domestic violence were more likely to explore the current offence, the impact of the offence on the victim, the significance of previous offending, the risk of harm to others and the offender's motivation to change. In domestic violence cases there was a greater willingness to draw conclusions about how seriously the offender viewed the offence and the risk of re-offending. In cases involving sexual offences there was more caution about drawing conclusions about the risk of re-offending. Reports on young offenders and women offenders were more likely to cover the subject's views of the consequences of the offence for themselves but less likely to cover the consequences for others.

Practitioners

4.18 **Practitioners** considered the provision of information and advice about offending to be highly relevant. They said they relied mainly on the offender to describe and explain the current offence and that it was often difficult to obtain a factually accurate picture. They thought that they would be able to deal better with this aspect of a report if they had access to more information relating to the offence from procurators fiscal. Some practitioners said that information of this kind was occasionally made available by local procurators fiscal in response to specific requests.

4.19 Practitioners also said they found it difficult to assess the risk of re-offending and risk of harm to others although they thought that it was crucial to the task of commenting on the feasibility of a community based disposal. They indicated that they were more likely to deal with the offender's feelings and views about the impact of the offence on any victim in more serious cases, for example, in cases of sexual abuse and assault. This kind of discussion was most effective when they had information about the impact from a separate source because offenders tended to minimise the harm they caused to victims.

Offenders

4.20 The majority of **offenders** said that the interview made them think about their offending and the reasons for it. This was triggered in most instances by simply talking about the offence. They said that social workers had rarely discussed the effects of the crime on any victim or the consequences of the crime for their families. Some offenders said that they had been caused to think about their offending when the issue was raised. About a third of offenders said that they had been selective in what they said about the current offence. A few offenders challenged the relevance of discussions about their previous offending.

Sentencers

4.21 **Sentencers** said that information and advice about offending and the offender's motivation to change could be useful. They did not find the information about the current offence which they presently received particularly helpful because it depended too much on the offender's version of events. They thought that assessing the likelihood of re-offending, the risk of harm to others and the offender's motivation to change was difficult and tended to rely on their own experience when they considered these issues. The information in reports about the current offence would be improved if it was more balanced and investigated the offender's attitude to the offence and its impact on others including any victim more thoroughly. The relevance of advice about the risk of re-offending, risk of harm to others and motivation to change would be improved if they could be clearer about the basis on which it was given.

CONCLUSIONS

4.22 The law does not require reports to include information about offending although the national standards stress its relevance. From the point of view of sentencers, this information appears to be most relevant when it does not duplicate information from elsewhere and when they consider that it is reliable. Practitioners emphasised its relevance but the analysis of the reports and the interviews with offenders showed that it was covered in a very variable way.

4.23 **We think that the subject of offending behaviour is central to the preparation of reports.** It is the reason for the court appearance and the report should contribute to the court's understanding of why the offence was committed, the extent to which the offender poses a risk if dealt with by a community based disposal and what the chances may be for preventing or reducing further offending. **The challenge for the service is how to improve the quality of this information and advice.**

4.24 The finding that offending behaviour was dealt with more comprehensively in cases involving domestic violence and sexual offences shows that good practice can be achieved. This appeared to be easier where more information about the nature of the offence and the circumstances surrounding it was available and the need to comment on certain aspects, including the risk of harm to others, more self-evident.

4.25 Sentencers want more than the offender's version of the current offence. Practitioners are presently given the complaint or indictment which provides information about what was alleged and proved and which is more detailed in some cases than in others. Beyond this, they rely in the main on what information they can glean from the offender who, as the interviews with offenders showed, may not be wholly frank. These interviews also found that practitioners tended not to probe a great deal into the attitudes and views of offenders about the effects and consequences of their crimes for themselves and others including their victims, a finding which was confirmed by the way the current offence was dealt with in a significant number of reports.

Improving practice

4.26 **Practice needs to improve.** First, practitioners should make better use of the information about the current offence and any previous convictions which they already have. Second, practitioners should improve their interviewing by drawing out more from offenders about their offending. Third, practitioners should have more information relating to the current offence and its impact on any victim where available. This would give them a better basis to probe offenders' explanations for and attitudes towards their offending.

4.27 To help with assessing the risk of re-offending, practitioners have access to information about any previous convictions from the procurator fiscal, the Scottish Criminal Records Office, or both. The Scottish Criminal Records Office record is more comprehensive and more useful. This information offers a basis for reviewing offending behaviour and, taken together with information about the offender's current offence, personality, social relationships and social circumstances, should help practitioners to reach an initial view about the risk of re-offending including the risk of harm to others. The need

D

to assess and comment on the risk of harm to others is not specified in the national standards although it can be inferred from the requirement to consider the risk of re-offending and offenders' views of the consequences of their offending for others including victims.

4.28 **By providing information and advice to the court about the risk of harm to others, social enquiry reports can make an important contribution to public safety.** Knowledge and skills in risk assessment are not yet well developed and much remains to be done to improve practice. We will address this issue when we next revise the supplement to the national standards on effective practice. The fact that the majority of the offenders interviewed said that talking about the offence made them think about their offending behaviour suggests that an impending court appearance may offer an opportunity for dialogue with offenders about the reasons why they offend and their motivation to change which is not yet fully exploited.

RECOMMENDATIONS

4.29 The Crown Office, the Scottish Court Service and local authorities should consider what can be done to increase the information given to practitioners about the current offence and its impact on the victim. This could be introduced in the first instance on a pilot basis for crimes/offences involving physical or psychological harm.

4.30 National standards should give greater attention to the contribution which social enquiry reports can make to public safety through the assessment of the risk of re-offending and harm to others.

4.31 Local authorities should make sure that practitioners make full use of the information which they receive about the current offence and any previous convictions.

4.32 Local authorities should evaluate the training requirements of staff to improve their skills in interviewing offenders about their offending and assessing the risk of re-offending and harm to others.

4.33 Local authorities should consider how best resources might be pooled to provide relevant training programmes most efficiently.

Chapter 5

How Reliable is the Information and Advice in Social Enquiry Reports?

5.1   The reliability of a report depends both on the range of information on which it draws and the extent to which this information is checked. The national standards set out the following information sources for practitioners to draw on[23]:

 – the complaint or indictment (the legal description of the offence being prosecuted);

 – the list of previous convictions which the procurator fiscal thinks are relevant for the sentencer to know about when sentencing;

 – the offender's full criminal record (provided by Scottish Criminal Records Office);

 – outstanding charges or warrants;

 – departmental records;

 – the offender;

 – the offender's family;

 – other people or organisations who may have relevant information, for example, medical practitioners and employers.

5.2   The standards state that practitioners must, where possible, contact the offender's family[24] and that other third parties, especially service agencies, should be contacted when the services which they provide form part of any course of action being proposed to the court[25].

Findings from the 410 full reports

5.3   All the practitioners responsible for preparing the 410 full reports had access to either the procurator fiscal's list of previous convictions or the Scottish Criminal Records Office record or both. Nearly all practitioners (98%) had access to the complaint or indictment.

---

23. National Standards, Part 2, paragraphs 35.1-8.
24. National Standards, Part 2, paragraph 53.
25. National Standards, Part 2, paragraph 49.3.

5.4   The percentages of reports which attributed information to the following sources are listed in Figure 2 below:

Figure 2: Percentages of reports containing information attributed to sources other than the offender & his/her family (N=40)

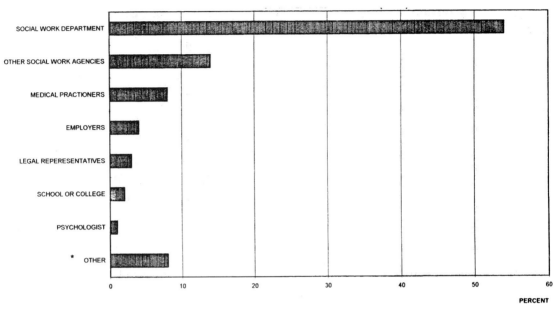

*ADDICTION SERVICES, HOUSING AGENCIES, THE ARMED FORCES AND REMAND CENTRES

5.5   The percentages varied for different types of offender and categories of offence. Information attributed to medical practitioners was found in 20% of the reports prepared on women; 63% of the reports where the subject was identified as suffering from a current mental health problem and 43% of reports where the subject was identified as suffering from a previous mental health problem. Reports prepared in cases of domestic violence also included a higher level of information attributed to medical practitioners (17%) and psychologists (8%).

Number of interviews

5.6   40% of reports were prepared on the basis of one interview. These interviews could involve the subject alone or the subject with his or her family. 33% of reports were prepared on the basis of 2 interviews involving the offender, the offender with his or her family or the family alone. The number of interviews was unclear in the remaining 27% of cases. Practitioners said that some reports could involve more than 2 interviews.

Home visits

5.7   It was clear that an interview had been conducted at home in 53% of the 410 reports but more home visits may have been undertaken which we could not identify.

Whether previously known to the social work department

5.8   31% of the subjects of reports were previously known to the social worker preparing the report; 30% were not and in the remaining 39% this information was not identifiable.

63% had had previous contact with social work departments. Of these, 34% had had contact as an adult, 20% as a child, and 46% as both an adult and a child.

Checking information

5.9   National standards do not offer precise guidance as to the kind of information which should be checked. Some of the information contained in reports, for example, the subject's age, sex and address is already known to the court from other sources, some information is supplied by the subject and not checked and some may be checked. We found that it was usually possible to tell the status of the information from the way practitioners phrased their reports. In one out of 5 reports, however, it was not clear whether some of the information was established fact, qualified fact or the report writer's opinion.

5.10   National standards say that information should be checked with third parties "where it is necessary for the preparation of the social enquiry report"[26]. They acknowledge confidentiality as an obstacle to checking information and outline procedures for practitioners to follow when an offender does not agree to a third party being approached to confirm or provide information.

5.11   We checked the information given to report writers about the current offence and any previous offending against the content of reports. In 56% of reports it was not clear whether the information about the current offence had been compared with the offender's account; in 16% it was not clear whether the information about any previous offending had been compared with the offender's account.

Practioners' views

5.12   **Practitioners** said that they drew routinely on the main information sources listed in the national standards. Whether they included information from other sources depended on the individual case. Information from a third party, for example, a medical practitioner, could be sought if an interview with an offender had raised a specific concern. Occasionally, the sentencer indicated that he or she wanted information from a particular source, for example, the victim in the case of domestic violence. When an action plan was put to the court as part of the community based sentencing proposal social workers tried to include additional information about the availability and suitability of resources.

Approaching third parties

5.13   Practitioners approached the task of seeking information from third parties, including other family members, in different ways. They normally sought the offender's consent before contacting a third party, although some said they sometimes told offenders that certain information would have to be checked. When the offender did not consent, most took the matter no further, although some offenders were asked why and the reasons included in the report. Some social workers said that they occasionally overruled the offender and approached a third party, usually after discussion with a line manager. Third parties were not always easy to contact within the time available.

---

26. National Standards, Part 2, paragraph 68.

5.14 They most frequently checked information:

- when there was a concern about an offender's health;
- when the offender said that he or she was attending treatment for a drug related problem;
- when verified information about the offender's circumstances, for example, the availability of work or suitable accommodation might tip the balance between a custodial and a non-custodial sentence; and
- when developing an action plan to put to the court.

Sentencers' views

5.15 **Sentencers** looked to reports in particular to provide and, where necessary, verify information about family circumstances, health, drug addiction, response to previous disposals and suitability for community based disposals. They used a range of other sources to obtain and check information including the defence agent, the procurator fiscal, voluntary agencies, medical reports, letters from employers and relatives in court.

5.16 They acknowledged that verifying information could take time and present problems for practitioners. The information which it was most important to check was information which had a direct bearing on disposal. This could include the subject's physical and mental health, the attitude of a partner who had been the subject of domestic violence or the availability of suitable community based resources. They were normally prepared to continue a case if information vital to disposal still required to be checked. As to their reliance on the report to verify specific items of information, sentencers placed mental health first, followed by available work, accommodation, available community based resources, physical health, income and disposable income. Sentencers considered that some of the information and advice which reports contained about the current offence, risk of re-offending and risk of harm to others was of questionable relevance because it could not always be relied on.

Offenders' views

5.17 **Offenders** were asked about contact with third parties to obtain or check information. Most did not object but wanted to be kept informed. A few thought it would have been helpful if others had been contacted although they had reservations about contact with employers because they did not want them to know that they were in trouble. Some offenders questioned the factual accuracy and therefore the reliability of some of the information in their reports.

CONCLUSIONS

5.18 **The objective for practitioners is to provide as reliable a report as possible within the time available.** This means making best use of information which is readily to hand and making sometimes difficult choices about what other information sources to pursue and what information to check. At present it is difficult for sentencers to assess the reliability of the information which reports contain because practitioners do not routinely indicate whom they have interviewed or contacted and what source documents they have drawn from.

Offending behaviour

5.19 Sentencers would rely more on the information about offending behaviour if more reports showed that the practitioner had checked the offender's account of his or her offending with the information received from procurators fiscal and the Scottish Criminal Records Office. Giving practitioners more information relating to the current offences would provide them with a better basis to discuss the offence with the offender and should enable them to report more objectively and reliably. Practitioners should have access to appropriate training to improve their assessment of offending behaviour including the risk of re-offending and risk of harm to others. This should improve the reliability of this aspect of assessment.

Home visits

5.20 National standards encourage report writers to contact the offender's family 'wherever possible' and to visit the offender's residence 'whether or not the offender lives with his or her family'. **We found the latter was not routinely done.** Practitioners gave a number of reasons for this. Foremost were concerns about personal safety, but other explanations included the subject's refusal to agree, that a visit was judged unnecessary and lack of time. A home visit may be an essential part of the assessment in some cases, for example, where it appears that current tensions in the family may have contributed to the offending behaviour and less essential in others, for example, where the offender is living alone in a bedsitter.

Second interviews

5.21 Although national standards do not oblige social workers to undertake a second interview with the offender, they set out a wide range of circumstances where a second interview "will normally be required". 40% of the main sample of reports were prepared on the basis on one interview. This may be because 31% of the subjects were already known to report writers. Other reasons may have been the time available, whether or not the subject was remanded in custody and the distance which either the social worker or the offender had to travel. Whatever the reasons, **we established a possible association between the number of interviews/contacts with the offender and his or her family and the quality of the report as assessed against criteria drawn from national standards.** The average number of interviews/contacts identifiable in all full reports was 1.15. The average for 'very good' reports was 1.57 and for 'poor' reports 1.04.

The issue of consent

5.22 **Some practitioners are limiting their freedom of action to seek or check information from third parties, including family members because they attach too much weight to obtaining the offender's consent.** The issue is not whether the offender consents but what the report writer thinks the court should know. Practitioners must decide whether information from a third party would strengthen the reliability and force of the report. In deciding, they should aim to be fair to the offender and sensitive to any possible adverse consequences. In fact, the findings from the interviews with offenders showed that they did not usually object to third parties being contacted provided that they were kept informed.

Medical information

5.23   We were surprised by the limited information attributed to medical practitioners in reports despite the high levels of ill-health which report writers identified[27]. The issue of the disclosure of confidential medical information in connection with the preparation of a social enquiry report is problematic. Medical information is normally provided only with the patient's consent and this principle applies equally to offenders. There are, however, some circumstances where it is necessary or desirable for doctors to disclose medical information without consent. These circumstances are outlined in a Code of Practice issued by The Scottish Office in 1990[28] and include:

– where disclosure is in the public interest;

– where disclosure is necessary to prevent serious injury or damage to the   health of a third party; and

– where disclosure is in the best interests of the patient.

5.24   The Scottish Office is currently preparing complementary guidance to this code of practice which will take account of the criminal justice social work context. As a general rule, social workers preparing reports should explain to the offender why they wish to approach a doctor and seek his or her consent before doing so. If the social worker thinks there may be a serious risk to others or to the offender the doctor may consider disclosing information without consent. Doctors are more likely to respond positively to a request for information if the social worker can be precise about the information they need, why they need it and what they will do with it. They are less likely to respond if the nature of the information and the reasons why it is sought are unclear.

Deciding what is important

5.25   There are limits to what information can be checked in the time available and sentencers and report writers agreed that it was most important to check information which had a direct bearing on disposal. It is impossible to predict what this information will be. Depending on the circumstances of each case, it could be, for example, health factors, disposable income, available community based resources, or the attitude of a spouse. In deciding what information to check, report writers must judge how important it is for the court to know that the information is reliable.

---

27. Appendix 3, paragraph 7.
28. Confidentiality of Personal Health Information Code of Practice, Scottish Home and Health Department 1990.

Checking with the offender

5.26 **We found that offenders were concerned about the factual accuracy of their reports.** Some reports are likely to contain inaccurate information. Offenders may question information provided by a third party which the report writer considers accurate. Offenders may not have understood the difference between facts and any conclusions which the report writer draws from them. For all these reasons, it is important that offenders should have the chance to say whether they think information in their reports is accurate.

RECOMMENDATIONS

5.27 National standards should make it clear that reports should state:

- whether the report writer already knew the subject;

- whether information from previous social work department records was used;

- how much information was available to the report writer about the current offence and any previous offending and whether this was checked with the offender's account;

- who was interviewed and how often;

- who else provided information and in what form;

- whether information critical to sentencing was checked; with whom and how confident the report writer is about its reliability.

5.28 National standards should set out criteria to assist practitioners to decide when a home visit is necessary. They should also set out those circumstances where a home visit would be unwise for reasons of personal safety.

5.29 National standards should make it clear that report writers should approach a third party, even if the offender objects, if they consider that the information is necessary to meet the needs of the court.

5.30 Practitioners should make sure that offenders have the opportunity to comment on the accuracy of the information about them in reports.

Chapter 6

Are Reports Written and Presented in an Appropriate Way?

Length, format and grammar

6.1   The 410 full reports were on average 3 pages long. Reports were nearly all divided into sections with headings. Few reports followed the sequence of headings set out in the national standards. One out of 10 reports contained errors of grammar, spelling or punctuation that we thought would affect their credibility.

6.2   The **sentencers** interviewed did not find reports too long although they thought that some information could be left out of some reports. They found the use of headings helpful and saw no reason for changing the way reports were set out. They liked reports which didn't use jargon.

The appropriateness of advice about disposal

6.3   The questionnaire asked **sentencers** to comment on whether they found it helpful for reports to include advice on specific sentencing options. The question attracted a wide spectrum of views. Those sentencers who found advice helpful gave as reasons that they needed to know what options were available or to know what probation was to address and how. They stressed that it was important that the reasons for suggesting a specific disposal were clear and the advice realistic. Those sentencers who were against the inclusion of advice on specific sentencing options argued that the advice which they received frequently did not allow for the gravity of the offence and tended to be biased in favour of the offender. Some sentencers considered that report writers were disadvantaged in considering possible options because of their limited access to information about the offence. A few simply thought it not appropriate for report writers to offer advice about sentencing. However on balance, the majority of sentencers were in favour of the inclusion of advice on specific sentencing options.

The format of advice about disposal

6.4   Sentencers were asked to give their preference for the format in which advice about disposal should be made from the following possible formats:

   a. a single sentencing option;

   b. a stated preference for one option amongst two or more possible options;

   c. a range of possible options;

   d. an option, or options, to be avoided.

6.5   Sentencers preferred advice which reviewed the pros and cons of a range of possible sentencing options. They also valued specific advice on options to be avoided. They were less happy for report writers to state their preference for a specific sentencing option either following a review of possible options or as a single 'recommendation'. The majority of those sentencers who were interviewed did not think it appropriate for reports to propose custody.

6.6   Approximately 40% of full reports concluded with a proposal or recommendation for a single sentencing option. The remaining 60% reviewed a range of sentencing options. 80% of reports in this latter group indicated a preference for one of these options and 40% referred to one or more options to be avoided.

6.7   **Practitioners** considered that providing advice about possible sentencing options was part of their job. There was no consensus about the format in which this advice should be set. It was important to build on the experience they gained of writing reports for particular sentencers. The extensive use of temporary and floating Sheriffs whom they often did not know, made this more difficult.

6.8   Some practitioners said that they avoided the word 'recommend' in their reports.

CONCLUSIONS

6.9   The majority of sentencers welcomed advice about possible sentencing options but were sensitive about framing it as a preference or recommendation. They preferred an open ended format setting out the pros and cons of various possible disposals. If a preference was stated it should be backed with good reasons. The guidance in the national standards is to make a single 'recommendation' wherever possible after reviewing the feasibility of several community based options. Practitioners used what they understood to be the preferences of individual sentencers to inform the way they gave advice. However cases were quite frequently dealt with by temporary and floating Sheriffs and the sentencer who requested the report did not always deal with the case. Practitioners also prepared reports for courts they did not know.

6.10   **The national standards rightly state that an important part of the job of the social worker is to provide information and advice about the feasibility of community based disposals, particularly where the offender may be facing custody.** This advice is intended to assist the court's wider consideration of suitability which must take more factors into account including the need for public protection and deterrence. Reports should assess the extent to which the offender constitutes a risk to others, whether this risk could be managed in the community without the need for a custodial sentence and whether there is a need for supervision afterwards if a custodial sentence is made[29]. Report writers should not take account of the need for deterrence which is properly the concern of the court. **We agree with the majority of those sentencers interviewed that it is not the task of social workers to propose custody.**

---

29.   The Supervised Release Order introduced in 1994.

6.11 If general agreement can be reached about the way in which social workers offer advice they will have to depend less on establishing the expectations of local sentencers and will be less vulnerable to possible criticism that their advice is 'unrealistic'. **The term 'recommendation' used by the national standards is not helpful.** We think the most appropriate form for advice is to review the pros and cons of specific sentencing options. Despite sentencers' preference for an open ended format, authors should be encouraged to state the community based option or options which **they** consider have the best chance of preventing or reducing offending, acknowledging that the court must take wider considerations into account. **If the author does not think that a given level of risk can be managed in the community he or she should say so.**

RECOMMENDATION

6.12 The national standards which deal with how to advise sentencers about disposal should be revised. In future, advice should take the form of a review of the pros and cons of several sentencing options. Where the author has a view about which community based option has the best chance of preventing or reducing offending, he or she should state it. If the author does not think that a given level of risk can be managed in the community her or she should say so.

Chapter 7

Is the Service Experienced as Fair?

7.1   Much of the information and advice included in reports is about the lives and behaviour of offenders and good quality reports should present these as accurately as possible. For the report writer, undertaking the report may be a routine task. For offenders, the request for a report means that they will be required to answer questions about themselves and the reasons for their offending which they may experience as intrusive. However, it also offers them an opportunity to talk to somebody undertaking an investigation on behalf of the court whose job it is to seek to understand and assess the reasons for their behaviour and what might be done to change it.

7.2   Offenders should always be treated fairly and given appropriate information. Are they properly briefed? Do they understand why certain questions are asked? Are they able to express a view about whether the information contained in reports is accurate? If the report suggests a particular sentencing option, do they know what it is? Do they know who will receive copies of the report written about them?

Offenders' views

7.3   The interviews conducted with the sample of 30 offenders showed that:

- most social workers discussed what they were going to write in their reports and what various disposals would entail;
- most offenders considered that they had been treated fairly at interview.

7.4   On a less positive note:

- very few offenders had absorbed much information about the purpose of their report, either from the sentencer or a court based social worker;
- few recalled receiving a leaflet from the social work department outlining the purpose of the report before their first interview;
- offenders remanded in custody for reports were given no advance notice of when they would be interviewed. They felt that this was not fair and that it had affected their response to the interview;
- not all offenders understood the relevance of some of the questions they were asked, particularly questions about personal or family matters;
- some offenders complained that some of the information contained in their reports was inaccurate;
- almost one third of offenders said they did not see a copy of the report before the case was dealt with (half of them said that they would have been prepared to go to the social work department office to do this if they had been offered the opportunity);

31

- offenders did not know whether they were entitled to keep a copy of the report and who would receive copies; and

- in two of the four inspection sites there was no up-to-date leaflet to give or send to the offender about what the report was for and how it would be prepared.

Sentencers' views

7.5   As the commissioners of reports, sentencers' views about the fairness of reports are equally important. We did not ask sentencers whether they thought reports were fair but the questionnaire and interviews allowed them to express their views about the impartiality of the advice which they received. Some sentencers thought that some of the information and advice which they received was less than wholly impartial because it gave too much weight to the views of offenders.

CONCLUSIONS

7.6   Offenders should be able to learn the content of their reports before the court hearing and be able to say whether they consider them factually accurate. They should know to whom copies will be sent and why. They should be able to retain a copy of their report and be told who will give one to them.

7.7   We think that some sentencers are right to say that the information and advice contained in some reports is not wholly impartial. Nevertheless, preparing a report is a complex task. Sentencers emphasise how important it is for a report to provide a "picture" of the offender. They rely on reports to tell them what offenders think about their offending and to describe the circumstances in which they live. In carrying out this kind of assessment, social workers are necessarily exposed to the views and life experiences of offenders at first hand and this contributes to their understanding about the reasons why they offend. It is possible that some sentencers see this as "bias" when arguably it derives from a closer appreciation of the reality of the lives of many offenders. **The task for practitioners is nevertheless to get as close to the truth as they can and it is not in the interest of the offender for the practitioner to accept what he or she says uncritically. The objective must always be to provide the court as far as possible with impartial information and advice.**

RECOMMENDATIONS

7.8   **Offenders remanded in custody whilst a social enquiry report is being prepared should be notified in advance of the purpose, date and time of interviews.**

7.9   **Offenders should be told who will see a copy of their report and why and should be able to retain a copy if they wish.**

Chapter 8

Is the Service Effective?

8.1   We approached the question of effectiveness by asking sentencers about the extent to which the service met their needs and by assessing the quality of the 410 full reports against the national standards.

Sentencers' views

8.2   **Sentencers** were very positive about the quality of the service. Nearly all said that it met their needs either "very well" or "quite well". Most considered that the service had improved either considerably or slightly since national standards were introduced (several sentencers said that they were unable to answer this question because they had been appointed since the introduction of national standards).

8.3   Sentencers made a number of suggestions about how reports could be improved. These were:

— more conciseness and cogency;

— better information about the current offence;

— avoiding "special pleading" for the subject of the report and the use of the term "client"; and

— including more information about the offender's views of the effect of the offence on the victim.

CONCLUSION

8.4   It was encouraging to learn that sentencers considered that the service met their needs well and that the introduction of national standards had led to improvements.

Did the reports meet national standards?

8.5   In order to give an overall rating to each report we derived the following **key indicators** from the national standards:

— using information sources other than the subject;

— verifying key information;

— making the status of information clear;

— analysing the current offence;

— analysing previous offending;

— assessing risk factors;

– assessing the offender's capacity and motivation to stop offending;

– providing information relevant to understanding offending;

– providing information relevant to sentencing;

– basing conclusions on evidence;

– arguing cogently for specific sentencing proposals ;

– including, where appropriate an action plan based on an understanding of offending behaviour; and

– being clear in style and presentation.

8.6   We rated the 410 full reports against these key indicators placing particular emphasis on identifying the main strengths and weaknesses of reports[30]. **On this basis we judged 8% to be 'very good', 55% to be 'quite good', 30% to be 'not very good' and 7% to be 'poor'.**

8.7   These findings show that slightly over 6 out of 10 reports generally conformed with national standards. The main strength of reports was in providing information about the offender which was relevant to understanding his or her offending or to sentencing. The main weakness of reports was in those aspects of report writing which required **analysis** (of the current offence and previous offending), **assessment** (of risk factors and the offender's motivation to stop offending) and the use of **evidence** (drawing from information sources other than the offender, reaching conclusions and making the case for a specific sentencing proposal).

8.8   Reports on certain types of offender and categories of offence varied from this overall pattern. Domestic violence cases were strong in their use of information sources apart from the subject; their analysis of the current offence; their assessment of risk factors; their provision of information relevant to sentencing; the cogency of their arguments for specific disposals and their inclusion of action plans based on an understanding of offending behaviour. Reports on sex offenders were also significantly better in the way they dealt with the current offence, risk factors and in the cogency of their arguments for specific proposals. Reports on offenders with current mental health problems scored significantly higher in their use of sources other than the subject.

8.9   As numbers were small (particularly the number of reports on sex offenders) this finding should be treated cautiously. **Nevertheless it appeared that good practice was more likely to be achieved in reports prepared on some types of offender and some categories of offence.** Many of the weaknesses we identified were also identified by sentencers, particularly dealing better with the current offence and ensuring that conclusions were linked to evidence and sentencing proposals cogently argued.

CONCLUSION

8.10 **The key indicators derived from the national standards provide a sound basis for assessing the quality of practice and it is encouraging that there was a substantial measure**

---

30. Reports were rated by an individual assessor but checks were made for inter-rater reliability.

of agreement between what sentencers thought constituted a good report and our own assessment. While sentencers responded positively to a general question about the quality of practice, we are concerned that nearly 4 out of 10 reports did not meet sufficient of the key indicators to conform with national standards. Managers and practitioners said that reports were being prepared to national standards and that the quality of reports was being monitored. Despite this, a substantial minority of reports was judged to be either "not very good" or "poor". Practice needs to be improved and these findings have implications for training staff and monitoring their practice.

RECOMMENDATION

8.11 Local authorities should use the key indicators set out at paragraph 8.5 as benchmarks for setting and monitoring the quality of practice.

Chapter 9

How Efficient is the Service?

9.1   **Sentencers** were broadly satisfied with the service which they received and did not raise any major concerns about its efficiency.

9.2   We asked them a series of questions about efficiency. Were all the reports required by law necessary? Were there occasions when they could indicate more precisely what information they needed in order to cut down the length of reports? Could a verbal report suffice more often? Were priorities for reports not required by law ever discussed? How well did liaison arrangements work?

The usefulness of reports required by law

9.3   Sentencers had mixed views about whether all the reports required by law were necessary. Their comments were qualified by the view that, to an extent, the value of a report depended on its quality whatever the sentencing option facing the court. Some questioned the value of requiring a report which was intended to contribute to the assessment of the feasibility of a community based disposal when the offender was facing a mandatory or virtually inevitable custodial sentence. Others said that the content of reports could be useful in helping the sentencer decide the length of a custodial sentence. Some mentioned the recently introduced supervised release order which enables the court to order a period of supervision following release from custody as a reason why a social enquiry report was almost always useful. There was therefore no general support for any change to the current position.

CONCLUSION

9.4   The lack of widespread support for change amongst sentencers suggests that the scope for reducing the number of reports required by law is not great. **To sentencers the usefulness of a report depends as much on its intrinsic quality as on the circumstances in which it is requested.** However, when custody is inevitable or virtually inevitable, we think it would be sensible for report writers to acknowledge this and to identify issues relating to the offender which should be addressed during a custodial sentence to improve his or her chances of living a crime free life on release. They should also comment on how serious a risk to the community the offender poses and whether a supervised release order may be warranted,. When offenders are sentenced to custody, their reports are forwarded to the prison and information of this kind could assist those providing services and planning for the offender's release during the period of imprisonment.

RECOMMENDATION

9.5   National standards should make it clear that when the offender is facing a likely custodial sentence, report writers should address the following questions:

– are there issues relating to the subject's offending which could help those providing services during a custodial sentence to work with the offender to reduce the risk?

– is there a need for supervision on release because of the risk which the offender may pose?

Pre-trial reports

9.6   The position with regard to reports prepared before trial was different. These reports are normally submitted to the High Court and are prepared whilst the accused is awaiting trial. If the accused has not indicated a guilty plea in advance, the report does not deal with the issue of offending behaviour.

9.7   **High Court Judges** were lukewarm about the usefulness of these reports. They had some use because of the background information which they provided but none of the five respondents considered them to be 'very useful' because they could not offer any information about the accused's offending behaviour. They said that they sometimes asked for a second report post-trial. Another suggested solution was to postpone the request for the report until after the verdict in cases going for trial. Our analysis of the 33 pre-trial reports included in the sample of 443 reports confirmed that they did not deal with issues of offending or provide any advice on disposal. As such they were not full social enquiry reports and could not be rated by the same criteria as the other reports.

9.8   **Practitioners** saw little value in pre-trial reports because they could not deal with offending behaviour. They also thought they were inefficient because the report might not be used and because the information was often out of date by the time the case was heard. This meant that the court not infrequently requested a post-trial social enquiry report.

CONCLUSION

9.9   **The case for retaining pre-trial reports where no advance plea of guilty has been made is not strong.** As a report is not used if the accused is found not guilty and as Judges may request an additional post-trial report which can provide more up-to-date background information and also deal with offending, there are built-in inefficiencies. Judges found them only moderately useful. Practitioners were frustrated because they were working to little apparent benefit.

RECOMMENDATION

9.10   **The practice of requesting pre-trial reports in High Court cases other than those covered by Section 76 of the Criminal Procedure (Scotland) Act 1995 should be discontinued.**

Shorter written reports

9.11   We explored the scope for shorter written reports. All **sentencers** commented that some reports contained extraneous information. However, the majority were not in favour of limiting reports to specified pieces of information and advice, other than in exceptional circumstances. They considered that reports should cover the ground and that there could be a danger of leading the author. More practically they pointed out that a different sentencer might deal with the case.

CONCLUSION

9.12 We appreciate sentencers' concerns that reports should provide as full a picture as possible. However, greater efficiency could be achieved if authors of reports had a clearer idea of any particular information needs at the point when a report was requested.. Two sentencers suggested that a checklist could be developed which they could complete and pass on when they requested a report. This idea is worth considering. The aim of such a checklist would be to guide but not determine the information to be included in a report.

RECOMMENDATION

9.13 **Social Work Services Group, local authorities and the Sheriff's Association should investigate the scope for developing a checklist which sentencers could use when requesting a report to indicate whether there are any particular issues which they wish the report to cover. The checklist should be piloted in one or more courts to evaluate its usefulness.**

Oral reports

9.14 Occasionally, **sentencers** asked court based social work staff to interview offenders at court to obtain or verify certain items of information. They considered, however, that the scope for using this kind of arrangement more often to reduce the number of requests for written reports was very small. They asked for oral reports in very specific situations or in emergencies. The lack of a written report had implications for any appeal. At one court, arrangements had been made to provide written information or advice on the same day and this had proved helpful. The practice had required the department and the court to overcome a number of logistical difficulties.

CONCLUSION

9.15 We agree with sentencers that the scope for increasing the use of oral reports is limited. Nevertheless, the fact that a brief written report could be provided on the day in one court shows that it is possible to deal with the sentencers' concern to have something in writing. It is worth considering this kind of arrangement if it avoids the need for a longer, more detailed report.

RECOMMENDATION

9.16 **Local authorities, in consultation with their local courts, should consider the scope for increasing efficiency by providing written reports at the point of conviction focused on specified items of information or advice where this would avoid the need for a full social enquiry report.**

Priorities for requesting reports

9.17   We asked **sentencers** if they agreed with the priorities for reports not required by law which are set out in the national standards[31] and if they had ever discussed these priorities with local service managers. The only priority which sentencers did not agree with was the low priority given to 'first or early offenders not at risk of custody'. They argued that in these cases a report had the potential to identify problems or difficulties in the lives or behaviour of offenders which, if resolved, could reduce the likelihood of future offending.

9.18   **Service managers** said that they had not yet used the national standards to discuss priorities for requesting social enquiry reports locally.

CONCLUSION

9.19   *Some sentencers were concerned not to overburden staff providing criminal justice social work services. There should therefore be scope for service managers and sentencers to discuss priorities for providing social enquiry reports locally using the priorities set out in the national standards.*

RECOMMENDATION

9.20   **Local authorities should discuss with sentencers locally priorities for providing social enquiry reports not required by law.**

Liaison

9.21   Most permanent Sheriffs knew about formal liaison arrangements and just over one third participated in liaison meetings. High Court Judges did not know about any formal liaison procedures and it was not possible for floating and temporary Sheriffs to participate in liaison. Sentencers in smaller courts were more likely to participate in liaison. In the largest court, responsibility for liaison was delegated to a small number of sentencers.

9.22   The extent to which **sentencers** gave social workers feedback about the service they received varied. It was given most frequently through discussion with individual practitioners and managers followed by meetings and written comments. Sentencers indicated that they did not always receive information about the range of available services from the local authority but that when they did it was most frequently in a leaflet or booklet.

9.23   We asked sentencers whether they had had an opportunity since 1 January 1994 to meet staff providing community based social work services to find out more about these services. Some sentencers did not answer this question. Those that did indicated that the most frequent contact was with staff providing intensive probation projects followed by bail information and community service. They reported comparatively little contact with staff providing supported accommodation and alcohol and drugs services. Some sentencers were offered opportunities to meet offenders who were undertaking community based

---

31.   Part 2, paragraphs 21.1-21.2.

disposals. A few sentencers who had not been offered these kinds of opportunities would have welcomed them.

9.24 Sentencers pointed out that liaison meetings required real issues to discuss. They thought that ways could be found to give practitioners more feedback about the reports they prepared (including probation and community service termination reports) if this was what practitioners wanted. They appreciated up-to-date information about services.

9.25 The four temporary and floating Sheriffs in our questionnaire sample estimated that over the 6 month period before they completed the questionnaire they had each sat in between 10 and 22 courts. Whilst the majority said that they were kept informed about the range of services at these courts, all acknowledged that they were only sometimes able to use the reports which they requested and that they were only usually or sometimes aware of any locally agreed priorities for providing social enquiry reports.

Managers and practitioners

9.26 **Managers and practitioners** underlined the potential value of liaison as a means of promoting, achieving and maintaining effective and efficient working relationships with sentencers. Senior staff undertook most of the formal liaison. Practitioners and junior managers said that they were not always kept informed about the agenda for and outcome of these meetings. They would have appreciated more opportunities to meet sentencers to review the service which they provided. Managers and practitioners pointed to some difficulties in developing and maintaining working relationships with temporary Sheriffs and to a lesser extent floating Sheriffs. Service plans and priorities were most likely to be raised at meetings arranged between Sheriffs and senior managers.

CONCLUSIONS

9.27 Local authorities should make sure that sentencers receive regularly updated information about services. This should include summaries of statistics which would inform sentencers about how the services they use are performing. This could provide a basis for discussing local service requirements and priorities.

9.28 Practitioners and managers would appreciate more regular opportunities to meet sentencers to review services. Meetings need a clear, mutually determined agenda which enables participants to discuss real concerns and find ways of dealing with them. Managers and practitioners appreciate it when sentencers show an interest in community based social work services. It is vital that managers encourage and make it as easy as possible for sentencers to learn at first-hand about the nature and scope of these services and that sentencers take up these opportunities. It is difficult to see how sentencers can make best use of the sentencing options available to them without a close knowledge of what they involve.

9.29 The extensive use of temporary and to a lesser extent floating Sheriffs in some local courts makes it harder for managers and practitioners to build working relationships. **Managers should make sure that temporary and floating Sheriffs are as fully briefed as possible about local services.**

RECOMMENDATION

9.30 Local authorities should make sure that arrangements for liaison with sentencers provide for the regular review of issues associated with the efficiency and effectiveness of services. Items for this agenda should include:
- priorities for reports not required by law;
- information for sentencers about the range of services available;
- the performance and targeting of services;
- the scope for increasing efficiency; and
- how the purposes of reports are best translated into practice, taking account of any revision to national standards.

The time allowed to prepare reports

9.31 **Practitioners** across the 4 inspection sites reported differences in the allowance managers made to calculate the time and associated costs of preparing a social enquiry report, the lowest being 4 hours and the highest 8 hours. Those practitioners who were allowed 4 hours felt strongly that this was not enough. A working party representing the Scottish Office and the Convention of Scottish Local Authorities[32] commissioned a study which concluded that the figure of 6.4 hours should be the average necessary for the purposes of financial and workload planning.

CONCLUSION

9.32 **A good quality report is the product of the competence of the author and the time available.** Reports will not all need the same time to prepare. For example, much will depend on whether the report writer already knows the offender and the extent of any travelling. The tasks involved include:
- preparing for a first interview by reading the referral, checking departmental records, going over information about the current offence and previous offending;
- arranging and conducting at least one interview;
- checking information with third parties where necessary;
- preparing and writing the report;
- checking the content of the report with the offender; and
- travelling to and from interviews where the offender is in custody or a home visit is made.

9.33 It is unlikely that a social worker can prepare and write a good report in 4 hours or less. We did not investigate the relationship between time and quality systematically, but we found that the relatively small number of reports which we rated as "very good" were based on more extensive contact with the offender and his or her family. We also found that the uptake of proposals for probation by the courts was higher when the proposal included an

---

32. SWSG/COSLA Workload Measures Group.

action plan. Conducting more interviews and preparing a detailed action plan take more time and restricting or reducing the average amount of time to prepare reports below that agreed by the Workload Measures Group convened by Social Work Services Group and the Convention of Scottish Local Authorities would be likely to affect their quality.

Administrative efficiency

9.34 **Practitioners** undertook the administrative work associated with preparing reports in a number of ways. Most reports were written in long hand and then typed. Relatively little use was made of personal computers.

9.35 Administrative systems for recording and sending out requests for reports and submitting completed reports to the court varied. **Managers** on one site said they could guarantee that a letter offering an appointment to the offender was issued either on the same day or by 10 00am the following day using a central computer with links to practice teams and a fax machine.

RECOMMENDATION

9.36 **Managers should examine whether social enquiry reports can be produced more efficiently by making more use of information technology.**

Service monitoring

9.37 **Managers** across the 4 inspection sites said they monitored quality in a range of ways. These included:

- requiring practitioners to monitor their practice;
- monitoring reports through supervision;
- examining samples of reports, for example, one in ten reports, reports prepared on particular categories of offenders, reports where the sentence was custody;
- asking sentencers to comment on the quality of reports;
- using monthly returns to review performance; and
- using information from the forms which authorities must complete for the Scottish Office to build up a national picture.

9.38 Although we did not investigate these methods in detail, we found that performance was monitored differently across the inspection sites. For example, in one site the manager saw all the reports which his staff prepared. In another, the manager had an 'unwritten contract' with his staff to speak to him if there were any difficulties. Statistics were collected and used in different ways. It was not always clear what criteria were being applied to assess quality. In one site, however, thorough monitoring appeared to be reflected in the high overall standard of reports.

CONCLUSION

9.39 **The finding that around 4 out of 10 reports fell short of national standards raises questions about how adequate monitoring is.** Some authorities monitored more systematically than others. The discrepancy between the amount of reported monitoring and the overall quality of reports suggests that managers should ask themselves whether the way they are monitoring is improving the quality of practice. Are the criteria sound? Are staff given proper feedback? Are steps taken to improve practice by providing relevant training opportunities?

RECOMMENDATION

9.40 **Local authorities should monitor the quality of social enquiry reports regularly according to criteria derived from the national standards.**

Chapter 10

Key Messages

10.1   In this chapter we summarise the key messages from this inspection.

The contribution of social enquiry reports to sentencing practice

10.2   We are in no doubt that social enquiry reports make a significant contribution to sentencing practice. Sentencers value them and are reluctant to see either the number or length of reports reduced. A well evidenced and argued case for a community based disposal can be persuasive. Good social enquiry reports do therefore help to achieve the objective set out in national standards that the courts do not use custody for want of a suitable community based disposal.

Improving reports

10.3   Whilst sentencers' comments about the overall quality of reports were positive, they identified some specific aspects of report writing which they thought could be improved. The most important of these was the need for greater detachment and objectivity and the avoidance of any "special pleading" on behalf of the offender.

10.4   **We believe that a considerable amount could be done to make reports more credible and relevant.** In particular, reports should deal better with offending and sharpen their focus on the risk of re-offending and harm to others. Since 1991 when national standards were issued, public concern about community safety and the risk to this safety posed by serious offenders has increased substantially. This is an issue which criminal justice social work practice cannot afford to ignore. In our view, reports should cover the seriousness and frequency of offending and report writers should be prepared to express a view about the risk of re-offending, particularly where it may involve the risk of harm to others. To do this, report writers must increase their knowledge and skills in risk assessment and we have made recommendations which address this issue. **For the future, we think that assessing the risk of re-offending and harm to others will be more central to writing reports than assessing the risk of custody.**

Value for money

10.5   While the courts appreciate the service which they receive, they do not pay for it. Set against the costs of other legal services, the costs of providing reports are comparatively modest. Sentencers are not keen to reduce the volume of reports or the amount of information which they contain. On the other hand, the demand for reports is already high and increasing whilst resources are limited. In these circumstances it is essential to find ways of improving efficiency. The following steps could make an impact:

- provide full reports for serious or persistent offenders and short reports for less serious and early offenders (if the court considers that a report is necessary at all);

- provide "same day" reports where a specific and limited piece of information or advice is required; and

- make greater use of personal computers and templates when preparing reports[33].

Local authorities should negotiate with their local courts about how changes of this kind could be implemented.

10.6 Another way of increasing value for money is for local authorities to consider deploying staff in different ways. Preparing a social enquiry report is a skilled task which requires the social worker to collect and sift information, to reach judgements and to engage with the offender to seek to motivate him or her to address his or her offending. Some staff will be better at this than others. It may make sense for some authorities at least to introduce more specialisation so that fewer social workers undertake more reports. This would make it easier to focus relevant training initiatives and would give staff more opportunities to use and enhance their practice skills.

National standards and quality

10.7 **National standards encourage good practice but cannot guarantee it.** Standards are not always followed. Some standards need to be revised. However detailed, standards do not replace the requirement for social workers to learn essential skills and to apply a critical intelligence and judgement in what they do. Preparing for and writing social enquiry reports demands skills of a high order. Standards can provide a framework but ultimately the ability of each worker ensures the quality of the service.

10.8 A number of factors outside the control of practitioners affect the quality of their work. Sentencers vary in their approach to sentencing and in their expectations of reports, making it difficult to reach a generally acceptable specification "of service quality"; social workers are examining the current offence on the basis of limited information; risk assessment is a specialist skill for which adequate training must be provided.

10.9 Nevertheless, authorities should be vigilant in finding ways to improve and assure quality. There is no one way of doing this and authorities should review routinely the way they monitor the service, the training and guidance available to staff, the contribution of supervision and peer review and the feedback which staff receive from sentencers and offenders.

Values in criminal justice social work practice

10.10 Social workers, like other professionals, practise within an ethical framework. The British Association of Social Workers has published a code of ethics[34], and the Central Council of Education and Training in Social Work requires students to demonstrate that

---

33. Recommended at paragraph 9.36.
34. A Code of Ethics for Social Work - British Association of Social Workers - last revised 1986 - currently under review.

they can apply professional values to their practice before qualifying[35]. The most commonly identified values are those of respect for the individual, a belief in the potential of each individual to change and develop and a commitment to social justice which challenges disadvantage and negative discrimination.

10.11 We have commented at various points in this report on the way in which social workers referred to the offenders on whom they prepared reports as their "clients". We take from this that they sought to apply their professional values primarily to their contact with the offender without considering the wider context of criminal justice. **We think this identification of the offender as "client" is inaccurate, misleading and explains why some sentencers were concerned that some reports were not sufficiently detached and objective.**

10.12 Social workers practising in the criminal justice setting have a professional responsibility towards the offenders with whom they work but must have equal regard for others involved in the criminal justice process including the victims of crime. In Scotland, the Association of Directors of Social Work (the professional association for social work managers) has issued a statement of values and principles[36] intended for criminal justice social work services. These focus on criminal justice social work concerns while reflecting the more general ethical stance of the profession. Points of emphasis include:

- seeing the offender as having some responsibility for his or her behaviour;

- recognising the appropriateness of external direction and control as a means of helping some offenders to learn to control themselves;

- acknowledging the needs and rights of the victims of crime including the right to be protected from the harm which some offenders may inflict;

- emphasising the desirability of effecting a reconciliation between the offender and society.

10.13 **Crime victims deserve more consideration within the criminal justice process and the risks which certain offenders pose to the community are matters of public concern.** Social workers preparing reports and working with offenders in the community must be alert to this and make sure their practice includes an awareness of the rights and needs of the victim and addresses issues of public safety. This position is supported by the Association of Directors of Social Work who have recently published a policy statement on the subject[37].

A sense of common purpose

10.14 The framework of law and national standards surrounding social enquiry reports allows for significant differences of view between individual sentencers and between sentencers and social workers about how the general purposes of reports are translated into practice. **This must reduce their efficiency and effectiveness.** There needs to be a clear understanding between the customer (sentencers) and the service provider (local

---

35. CCETSW, Paper 30, revised 1995.
36. Issued by the Association of Directors of Social Work.
37. ADSW Policy Statement on Victims of Crime, February 1996.

authorities) and Government about how the general purposes of reports should be translated into practice. Achieving this will require frank and focused discussion between sentencers and service providers locally and between the representatives of Government, sentencers and service providers nationally on the issues which we have raised and on our recommendations to improve the quality of the service.

Chapter 11

Comment of Lay Inspectors

11.1 We were pleased to have the opportunity of participating in this inspection, and wish to express our appreciation to the full-time members of the team for their guidance and co-operation.

11.2 We were fully involved in the preparation of this report and endorse all the findings and recommendations. However, on the basis of our own backgrounds and experience, there are several points which we would particularly like to stress.

11.3 Our role as lay inspectors proved both interesting and challenging and we believe that we made a useful contribution to this important inspection. We hope that the use of lay inspectors will be a feature of future social work inspections.

11.4 **Comments by Tom Buyers, OBE**

Mr Buyers spent most of his working life in the oil industry; from 1985 to 1989 he was HM Chief Inspector of Prisons for Scotland. He is currently involved in the voluntary sector.

"Based on my experience of the penal system, I have little doubt that even in the best regimes, custody is damaging for many offenders. The cost is high and most prisoners re-offend after release, especially the younger men who make up a large proportion of the prison population. In contrast, non-custodial sentences are much less costly and offer better opportunity for improvement in social responsibility. Provided there is no significant danger to the community, such disposals must be the preferred option.

The decision whether to impose a custodial or non-custodial sentence is therefore crucial in many cases, with long-term implications both for the offender and for society at large. To reach the decision the sentencer has to take all aspects into account, but clearly the social enquiry report can be a key factor. However, to achieve its full potential the report must be well-balanced, with clear analysis, logical conclusions and a plan for a community-based disposal where appropriate. I therefore strongly support our recommendations for the additional training of practitioners, improved monitoring procedures and enhanced efficiency in the production of reports.

The question of resources must also be considered; sentencers should be aware that over use of the system could result in a loss of quality; social work managers should ensure that report writers have sufficient time allocated to meet the exacting standards required; and resources should be available to provide the community based disposals needed. Resources so deployed are likely to be much more cost-effective than in the provision of more penal establishments.

There are two other matters described in our report which I would like to stress. First, the question of contact between the social workers who prepare the reports and the sentencers who ask for the reports and subsequently use them. The two parties may rarely meet, and indeed may hardly know each other; and there is often little opportunity for feedback. In any field of activity, good contacts between the provider of a service and the user of that service are essential if the service is to develop and improve.

The second point arises from my involvement in the discussions with offenders who had been the subject of social enquiry reports. Many stated that the interview with the social worker had been helpful to them; confronted with their anti-social behaviour, they began to realise how damaging it had been both for themselves and other people. The interview may be a first step in the process of rehabilitation for some, and in this respect the social worker has a dual role in preparing the report. This aspect should be recognised by all those involved."

11.5 Comments by Joan Kavanagh

Joan Kavanagh has a background in education and experience as a member of a children's panel, a mediation and reparation project and victim support.

"For me, taking part in the inspection and preparing the report on our findings was a voyage of discovery and required a steep learning curve.

Against this newly acquired background, it seems to me almost impossible to exaggerate the importance of the social enquiry report because it is a bridge between the sentencer and the offender of whom it provides a snapshot in his reality and potential for change. It is the means also by which a community based punishment can be explored and thus reduce the use of custody, which is expensive (I believe it to be in the region of £27,000 per year per person) while its effectiveness in rehabilitating offenders is open to question.

The preparation of a social enquiry report is a highly complex and skilled activity. I, therefore, wholeheartedly subscribe to all the report's recommendations about supporting social workers in this crucial task. Especially urgent is the need to establish a common frame of reference for sentencers and social workers in the production of these reports. Without open and frank communication between these two, the degree of incoherence which I detected in the system, is likely to continue and undermine the quality of the reports.

Three encouraging findings emerged from the inspection:

- the sentencers were satisfied with the service they received from the social workers;
- a majority of offenders found the process and the reports themselves fair;
- social workers identified the changes needed to improve their performance.

I was, however, disappointed to find that social enquiry reports lack a victim perspective. Many social workers were aware of this and some admitted that victims were still marginalised. I formed the distinct impression that sentencers were looking for more information about the effect of the crime on the victim. Of particular concern to me was the absence of information from any source, where the offender has pleaded guilty and there is no trial, as to the effect of the offence on the victim. Having been involved with victims in three such cases, I recognise the sense of injustice that such victims feel. That the victim's perspective should be fairly represented in the criminal justice system would, I imagine, receive widespread support in the community.

It was heartening to find that two groups of social workers whom I consulted, backed the concept of restorative justice and were in favour of mediation and reparation schemes. Such schemes enhance the position of the victim and provide a means of healing, while enabling the offender to be reconciled to the community.

One of the most demanding tasks of the inspection was the grading of social enquiry reports and what they revealed about the offenders distressed me. It was disturbing to read of so many young people in trouble with the law, many from broken or difficult homes, with few or no educational qualifications, unemployed and with little realistic hope of being so. I say more: it seemed to me that individual responsibility (in which I believe) was over-emphasised in assessing offenders when they were effectively prevented from participating in our society or for re-entry into it after a prison sentence.

The inspection gathered and analysed offenders' perceptions of social enquiry reports for the first time. These volunteers did so for two reasons. Firstly, 'to have their say' and, secondly 'to help other people who would have social enquiry reports written about them'. They obviously cared deeply about their reports and some spoke warmly of the social workers who wrote them. In particular, offenders wanted to see their reports before going to court for sentence. As one offender put it: ' I was raging because I didn't see my report before the court hearing'. I would have felt the same! It was reassuring to learn that other offenders had found the whole process, though fraught, 'helpful' and one 'life-enhancing'.

My experience in taking part in this inspection has confirmed me in my view that the criminal justice system, as presently constituted, is a blunt instrument for providing justice for either victims or offenders. It has also reinforced me in my belief that the best hope for offenders lies in challenging and positive relationships with other people. Probation, community service, rehabilitative regimes in prisons and after care look like the best options for them and for us in the community.

In this connection, I was disappointed to learn that some sentencers did not visit as a matter of course community service schemes, prisons (except for formal visits) nor intensive probation projects.

This inspection and subsequent report-writing I found both challenging and rewarding. It gave me a privileged insight into a world of which I previously knew little. It was always a pleasure to work with the civil servants and their ancillary staff in our team whose good humour, tolerance and courtesy were exemplary."

List of Recommendations

For Local Authorities

1.   Local authorities should make sure that social workers:

- send every offender on whom a report is requested a leaflet about the   purpose of a social enquiry report and what is involved;

- explain to offenders what reports are for and that they include an assessment of offending behaviour and what can be done to reduce the risk of further offending; and

- check that offenders understand.

(paragraph 3.16)

2.   Local authorities should give members of the legal profession likely to act as defence agents the same information about reports that they give to offenders (paragraph 3.17).

3.   Practitioners should explain to the subjects of reports why they are asking them questions about themselves and their circumstances (paragraph 4.12).

4.   Local authorities should ensure that the staff who prepare reports are appropriately trained to:

- interview offenders about their finances, their health, their use of alcohol and other drugs; and

- use this information in a relevant way in reports.

(paragraph 4.13)

5.   Local authorities should make sure that practitioners make full use of the information which they receive about the current offence and any previous convictions (paragraph 4.31).

6.   Local authorities should evaluate the training requirements of staff to improve their skills in interviewing offenders about their offending and assessing the risk of re-offending and harm to others (paragraph 4.32).

7.   Local authorities should consider how best resources might be pooled to provide relevant training programmes most efficiently (paragraph 4.33).

8. Practitioners should make sure that offenders have the opportunity to comment on the accuracy of the information about them in reports (paragraph 5.30).

9. Offenders remanded in custody whilst a social enquiry report is being prepared should be notified in advance of the purpose, date and time of interviews (paragraph 7.8).

10. Offenders should be told who will see a copy of their report and why and should be able to retain a copy if they wish (paragraph 7.9).

11. Local authorities should use the key indicators set out at paragraph 8.5 as benchmarks for setting and monitoring the quality of practice (paragraph 8.11).

12. Local authorities, in consultation with their local courts, should consider the scope for increasing efficiency by providing written reports at the point of conviction focused on specified items of information or advice where this would avoid the need for a full social enquiry report (paragraph 9.16).

13. Local authorities should discuss with sentencers locally priorities for providing social enquiry reports not required by law (paragraph 9.20).

14. Local authorities should make sure that arrangements for liaison with sentencers provide for the regular review of issues associated with the efficiency and effectiveness of services. Items for this agenda should include:

- priorities for reports not required by law;

- information for sentencers about the range of services available;

- the performance and targeting of services;

- the scope for increasing efficiency; and

- how the purposes of reports are best translated into practice, taking account of any revision to national standards.

(paragraph 9.30)

15. Managers should examine whether social enquiry reports can be produced more efficiently by making more use of information technology (paragraph 9.36).

16. Local authorities should monitor the quality of social enquiry reports regularly according to criteria derived from the national standards (paragraph 9.40).

For National Standards

17. When national standards are next reviewed, members of the judiciary should be consulted about how the general purposes of social enquiry reports should be translated into practice (paragraph 3.15).

18.   National standards should give greater attention to the contribution which social enquiry reports can make to public safety through the assessment of the risk of re-offending and harm to others (paragraph 4.30).

19.   National standards should make it clear that reports should state:

- whether the report writer already knew the subject;

- whether information from previous social work department records was used;

- how much information was available to the report writer about the current offence and any previous offending and whether this was checked with the offender's account;

- who was interviewed and how often;

- who else provided information and in what form;

- whether information critical to sentencing was checked; with whom and how confident the report writer is about its reliability.

(paragraph 5.27)

20.   National standards should set out criteria to assist practitioners to decide when a home visit is necessary. They should also set out those circumstances where a home visit would be unwise for reasons of personal safety (paragraph 5.28).

21.   National standards should make it clear that report writers should approach a third party, even if the offender objects, if they consider that the information is necessary to meet the information needs of the court (paragraph 5.29).

22.   The national standards which deal with how to advise sentencers about disposal should be revised. In future, advice should take the form of a review of the pros and cons of several sentencing options. Where the author has a view about which community based option has the best chance of preventing or reducing offending, he or she should state it. If the author does not think that a given level of risk can be managed in the community her or she should say so (paragraph 6.12).

23.   National standards should make it clear that when the offender is facing a likely custodial sentence, report writers should address the following questions:

- are there issues relating to the subject's offending which could help those providing services during a custodial sentence to work with the offender to reduce the risk of re-offending on release?;

- is there a need for supervision on release because of the risk which the offender may pose?

(paragraph 9.5)

For the Scottish Court Service

24.   The practice of requesting pre-trial reports in High Court cases other than those covered by Section 76 of the Criminal Procedure (Scotland) Act 1995 should be discontinued (paragraph 9.10).

For the Scottish Office, Local Authorities and the Sheriffs' Association

25.   SWSG, local authorities and the Sheriff's Association should investigate the scope for developing a checklist which sentencers could use when requesting a report to indicate whether there are any particular issues which they wish the report to cover. The checklist should be piloted in one or more courts to evaluate its usefulness (paragraph 9.13).

For the Crown Office, Scottish Court Service and Local Authorities

26.   The Crown Office, the Scottish Court Service and local authorities should consider what can be done to increase the information given to practitioners about the current offence and its impact on the victim. This could be introduced in the first instance on a pilot basis for crimes/offences involving physical or psychological harm (paragraph 4.29).

APPENDIX I

Members of the inspection team were:

Felim O'Leary	Inspection Manager
John Waterhouse	Lead Inspector
Val Cox	Inspector
Laurie Naumann	Inspector
Tom Buyers	Lay Inspector
Joan Kavanagh	Lay Inspector
Anna Thomson	Administrator
Allison Todd	Administrator

The following experienced social workers helped to rate the sample of social enquiry reports:

John Fleming	formerly Strathclyde Region
Drew Hall	formerly Strathclyde Region
David Watts	formerly Tayside Region
Ray Myers	formerly Fife Region

Membership of the Inspection Advisory Group was:

David Affleck	nominated by Association of Directors of Social Work
Sheriff Richard Scott	nominated by the Sheriff's Association
Dr Fiona Paterson	SOHD, Central Research Unit
Lesley Clare	SOHD, Social Work Services Group, Division 1
Colin Reeves	SOHD, Criminal Justice and Licensing, Division IIB
Eric Cumming	Scottish Court Services
Bill Gilchrist	Crown Office

Vivienne Campbell carried out and wrote up the interviews with offenders.

Anne Manners typed the report.

APPENDIX 2

Profile of the Subjects of Reports

Who are the subjects of reports?

1.   We collated and analysed information from the sample of 443 reports to build up a picture of the main characteristics of the subject of reports.

Personal Characteristics

2.   Most were male (89%) and aged between 16 and 25 (65%). A very small number were over 60.

3.   Most were single (66%). Just over one fifth were married or co-habiting (22%), the remainder were separated, widowed or divorced.

4.   Most were unemployed (62%). Just over one fifth (22%) were employed or self-employed. Relatively small numbers were in some form of educational training (7%).

5.   Just over half lived with parents/relatives or friends (55%). 23% lived with a partner/family and 10% alone. 3% were living in specialist supported accommodation and 6% were homeless.

6.   25% had been subject to compulsory measures of care as a child and nearly one half of these had been in residential care at some point.

7.   A considerable amount of ill-health was reported. 5% were categorised as "long-term sick", 9% had been treated for a mental health problem in the past and 5% were receiving treatment. In addition, a substantial number of other illnesses and disabilities was mentioned.

Offending Behaviour

8.   The main crime or offence was dishonesty (62%), this was followed by crimes and offences involving violence (21%), breach of the peace (14%), road traffic offences (10%), drug offences (5%) and sexual offences (2%).

9.   74% of the sample had previous convictions. The average number of previous convictions libelled by the procurator fiscal was 11 and the average number cited in the Scottish Criminal Records Office record was 15 (the Scottish Criminal Records Office figure includes convictions related to breach of bail requirements which were often proved at the same time as the main crime/offence).

10.   Nearly half (47%) had served one or more custodial sentences. 54% had already been the subject of a probation order and 48% subject of a community service order.

11.   We checked this information against the information contained in the national statistics which drew from a much larger sample of reports (4,832 reports prepared during the first 3 months of 1994). The main differences were in the percentages of those who had previously been sentenced to custody, probation and community service and in the percentage who were previously subject to compulsory measures of care; all of which were significantly lower in the national statistics. We are not clear about the reasons for this discrepancy because we do not know the basis on which report writers completed the national statistical returns.

12.   **On the basis of this information we can say that the subject of a report is most typically an unmarried young man aged between 16 and 25 who is unemployed and living at home. He left school at 16 with few, if any, formal qualifications. There is a distinct possibility that he was subject to compulsory measures of care as a child. His crime is likely to be one of dishonesty and he will have a considerable number of previous court appearances. If the crime or offence was not one of dishonesty it probably involved violence, public disorder or motor vehicles. He may have already served a custodial sentence and been placed on probation or community service.**